# TABLE OF CONTENTS

# Introduction

## What is Iced Coffee?

While coffee really needs no introduction, let's simply define it for formality's sake. Coffee is a brewed beverage prepared from the roasted seeds of the coffee plant. Normally, this beverage is served hot, and has a bitter and acidic flavor when no additives are added to the brew. Due to a chemical in coffee, caffeine, the beverage has a stimulating effect on humans. Coffee, along with all its very numerous variations, is one of the most consumed beverages in any part of the world.

Iced coffee often refers to a variation of coffee that is served cold. As with its traditional form, iced coffee has also gained wide acceptance all around the world. Several variations of iced coffee exist in different countries including Australia, Canada, Chile, Germany, Greece, India, Israel, Italy, Japan, Philippines, Saudi Arabia, Thailand, United Kingdom, United States, and Vietnam. Some of these variations are quite simple, while others are fairly extravagant. These variations have also been said to be reflective of the culture, palate, and climate of the country of origin.

There are actually several fairly common ways to prepare iced coffee. The most obvious is to simply serve hot-brewed coffee cold. However, this may also leave a very bitter taste in the end product. A better way, according to some coffee aficionados is to cold brew. Cold brewing actually takes quite a bit of time. This is done by leaving ground coffee to soak for several hours in water, and then filtering the resulting mixture. The entire system relies mainly on time, rather than heat, to infuse the flavor of the coffee in the water. The upside to cold brewing though is that does not leave the harsh and bitter taste the traditional method does. Nonetheless, in more commercial settings cold brewing is not that popular. This is simply because of the vast amount of time involved to produce very small amounts of the finished product. The most common commercial method is to use a strong shot of espresso to dissolve the additives and flavorings. This flavored espresso is then poured directly into ice-cold milk and served with ice cubes.

## Iced Coffee Recipes

Throughout this report, we shall discuss some of the quick, easy, and delicious ways of making iced coffee. Although some of these recipes may seem fairly common, there are also others that are quite quirky and require a more open mind to fully appreciate! After all, you obviously didn't buy this report just to learn about the recipes that you could have easily figured out on your own, did you?

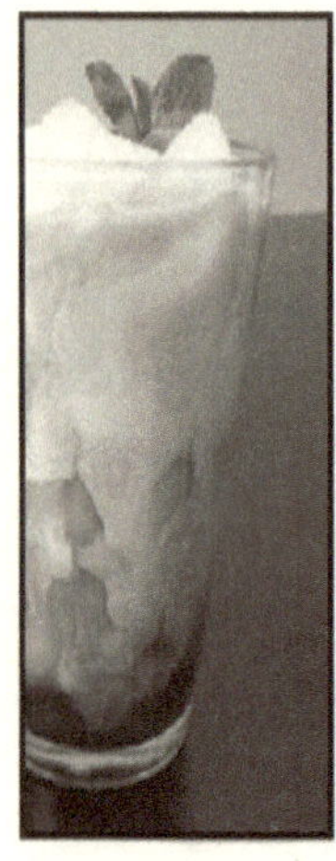

## SPICY THAI ICED COFFEE

Ingredients:

- 2 cups of crushed ice
- 2 teaspoons of grounded black cardamom
- 1 teaspoon of almond extract
- 6 tablespoons of grounded coffee
- 2 tablespoons of heavy cream
- 2 tablespoons of sugar

Preparation:
1.    Blend the ground coffee and black cardamom together.
2.    Use this blend to brew a pot of coffee.
3.    Add the sugar and almond to the brewed coffee.
4.    Stir.
5.    Put the brewed coffee in the fridge until fully chilled.
6.    Divide the crushed ice into 4 tall glasses.
7.    Pour the chilled coffee in the glasses.
8.    Add half a spoon of cream to each glass.
9.    Serve and sip slowly.

# VIETNAMESE ICED COFFEE

Ingredients:

- 2 cups of ice cubes
- ½ cup of sweetened condensed milk

- 3 cups of hot brewed coffee or espresso

Preparation:
1. Place a generous amount of ice cubes in a tall glass.
2. Pour 2 tablespoons of the condensed milk in the glass.
3. Pour in some of the coffee or espresso.
4. Stir briskly with a long-handled spoon.
5. Repeat steps 1 thru 4 to make 5 servings in total.
6. Serve each glass with a straw.
7. Share with friends!

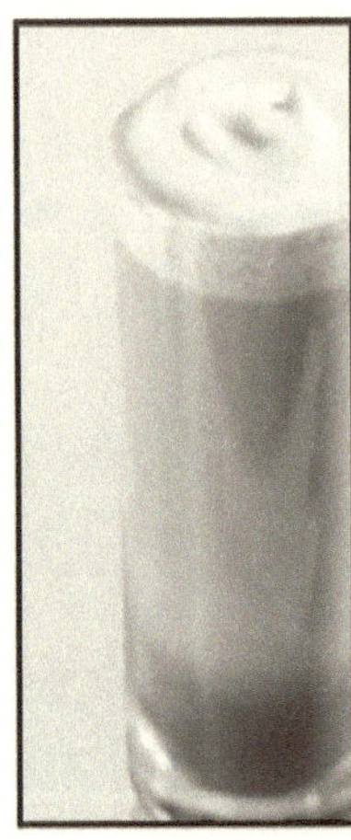

## **GREEK FRAPPE**

Ingredients:

- 1 tsp. instant coffee
- 1 cup cold water
- 1 tsp. brown sugar
- Cream to taste
- Ice cubes
- Whipped cream, chocolate sprinkles, or other optional toppings

Preparation:
1.    Place the instant coffee, cold water, brown sugar, and cream into a shaker.
2.    Shake vigorously until it produces very thick foam. Alternatively, you can use an electronic hand mixer to create richer more consistent foam.
3.    In a tall glass, place a number of ice cubes to your preference.
4.    Pour the mixture on top of the ice cubes.
5.    Add your preference of optional toppings.
6.    Add a straw or serve directly.
7.    Enjoy!

# CHAI GRANITA

Ingredients:

- 3 tablespoons of powdered chai tea mix
- 2 tablespoons of dark chocolate syrup
- 1 cup of cold coffee
- 1 can of whipped cream

Preparation:
1. Thoroughly mix all ingredients in a shallow container.
2. Cover the container with a lid or plastic wrap.
3. Place the container in a freezer for at least an hour.
4. Use a fork to scrape through the mixture.
5. Repeat step 4 every 50 minutes until the mixture is completely frozen.
6. Top with whipped cream.
7. Serve immediately!

# WHITE MOCHA GRANITA

Ingredients:

- 3 tablespoons of white chocolate syrup
- ½ cup of milk
- 1 cup of cold coffee

Preparation:
1. Pour the coffee and milk in a dish.
2. Thoroughly mix in the syrup.
3. Place the dish in the freezer.
4. Let it chill for 1 hour.
5. Scrape a fork through the mixture every 45 minutes until it is fully frozen.
6. Optional. Scrape less for a chunky mixture; scrape more for a smooth mixture.
7. Scrape the frozen mixture one more time before serving.

# CHOCOLATE AND COFFEE MARTINI

Ingredients:

- 1 tablespoon of vodka
- 2 tablespoons of chocolate liqueur
- 2 ½ tablespoons of Bailey's Irish Cream liqueur
- 4 tablespoons of cold brewed coffee
- 1 scoop of any chocolate ice cream

Preparation:
1.    Pour the Irish Cream in a martini glass.
2.    Pour the chocolate liqueur, then the vodka.
3.    Pour the coffee. You will notice you have created beautiful layers with the mixture.

4.    Top with the ice cream.
5.    Immediately serve.

# MINTY CHOCO MARTINI

Ingredients:

- 5 ice cubes
- 2 tablespoons of vodka
- 2 tablespoons of chocolate-mint cocktail mix
- 1 tablespoon of Kahlua or coffee-flavored tequila or any other coffee liqueur
- 1 tablespoon of brewed coffee

Preparation:
1. Combine all the ingredients in a cocktail shaker.
2. Shake until water starts condensing on the outside of the cocktail shaker.
3. Strain the mixture in a martini glass.
4. Serve with a green martini umbrella or with decorative mint leaves.

# GINGER COFFEE COCKTAIL

Ingredients:

- 3 ice cubes
- 1 cup of semi-packed brown sugar
- 1 cup of water
- 1 sliced piece of ginger, peeled
- 4 tablespoons of coffee-flavored tequila
- 1 finely crushed gingerbread

Preparation:
1. Combine the sugar and ginger in a saucepan.
2. Boil in water for 30 minutes.
3. Remove the saucepan from the stove.
4. Strain the ginger.
5. Allow the mixture to cool in a container.
6. Chill for 30 minutes.
7. Combine the chilled mixture with the tequila in a cocktail shaker.
8. Shake thoroughly.
9. Strain the cocktail in a small glass.
10. Top with the crushed gingerbread
11. Serve on the rocks.

# CARAMEL AND CINNAMON ICED COFFEE

Ingredients:

- 3 ice cubes
- ½ teaspoon of cinnamon
- ½ cup of caramel syrup
- 6 tablespoons of ground coffee

Preparation:
1. Mix the cinnamon and ground coffee.
2. Brew a pot of coffee using this mixture.
3. After the coffee is done brewing, add the caramel syrup.
4. Stir thoroughly.
5. Chill in the fridge for an hour.
6. Pour the chilled coffee in a glass.
7. Place the ice cubes in the glass.
8. Use any extra caramel syrup to decorate the top.
9. Serve!

# HONEY ICED COFFEE

Ingredients:

- 1 cup of ice cubes
- 4 cups of milk
- ¼ cup of honey
- ¼ cup of boiling water
- ¾ cup of cold water
- 2 tablespoons of instant coffee

Preparation:
1. Dissolve the instant coffee in boiling water.
2. Pour the honey.
3. Mix well.
4. Add cold water.
5. Pour the mixture in 4 glasses with ice.
6. Top off 1 cup of milk for each glass.
7. Enjoy!

# ICED café AU LAIT (ICED MILK COFFEE)

Ingredients:

- 2 cups of crushed ice
- 2 ¼ cups of cold coffee
- 2 cups of milk

Preparation:
1. Slightly mix the milk and cold coffee.
2. Pour the mixture with the crushed ice in a blender.
3. Blend until mixture turns frothy.
4. Serve immediately.

# NUTTY ALMOND ICED COFFEE

Ingredients:

- 12 ice cubes
- 1 teaspoon of vanilla extract
- ½ teaspoon of almond extract
- 3 teaspoons of sugar
- 2 cups of coffee
- 2 cups of milk
- 1 can of whipped cream
- 2 teaspoons of chopped almonds

Preparation:
1. Mix the milk and coffee in a tall pitcher.
2. Pour in the sugar and vanilla extract.
3. Add the almond extract.
4. Mix well.
5. Pour mixture into 4 glasses.
6. Put 3 ice cubes in each glass.
7. Add whipped cream if desired.
8. Top off with the chopped almonds.
9. Serve!

# TOFFEE YUMMY ICED COFFEE

Ingredients:

- 1 shot of espresso
- ¼ cup of toffee
- 2 scoops of vanilla ice cream

Preparation:
1. Chop the toffee.
2. Put the espresso and ice cream in a blender.
3. Blend until smooth.
4. Pour mixture in a glass.
5. Top it off with the chopped toffee.
6. Serve immediately with a spoon.

# FRESH LEMON ICED COFFEE

Ingredients:

- 4 tablespoons of sherbet lemon
- ½ teaspoon of lemon juice
- 1 teaspoon of grated lemon rind
- 1 teaspoon of sugar
- ¼ cup of coffee

Preparation:
1. Quickly mix all the lemon ingredients in a bowl.
2. Pour the sugar and coffee in a blender along with the lemon mixture.
3. Blend until smooth.
4. Pour in a chilled glass with ice.
5. Serve with a slice of lemon dipped in the coffee or decorated at the side.

# EGGNOG ICED COFFEE

Ingredients:

- 2 cups of cold milk
- 2 cups of cold coffee
- 4 tablespoons of sugar
- 2 tablespoons of nutmeg
- 4 eggs

Preparation:
1. Beat the eggs and sugar together in a bowl.
2. Whisk in the coffee and milk.
3. Chill.
4. Pour the chilled mixture in a glass.
5. Sprinkle some nutmeg on top.
6. Serves 4.

# RASPBERRY CAPPUCINO

Ingredients:

* 4 ice cubes
*  1 cup of milk
* 1 cup of hot coffee
* 1 or ½ shot of espresso
* 1 tablespoon of chocolate syrup
* 1 tablespoon of raspberry syrup
* 2 whole raspberries

Preparation:
1. Combine both syrups in the hot coffee.
2. Stir well until the syrups dissolve.
3. Pour the milk onto the coffee.
4. Put the mixture in the fridge until fully chilled.
5. Put the ice cubes in a tall glass.
6. Pour the chilled mixture over the ice cubes.
7. Put in the raspberries.
8. Drink slowly.

# COKE FLOAT SURPRISE

Ingredients:

- 1 can of coca-cola
- !T cup of light cream
- 2 ½ cups of coffee
- 4 scoops of coffee-flavored ice cream

Preparation:
1. Mix the light cream and the coffee.
2. Pour the mixture into 4 glasses, each one half full.
3. Top each glass with the ice cream.
4. Divide the can of coca-cola in each glass.
5. Enjoy!

# CHOCO-LOCO

Ingredients:

- 2 teaspoons of powdered malt
- 3 teaspoons of powdered cocoa
- 6 teaspoons of instant coffee
- 1 tablespoon of chocolate ice cream
- ¼ cup of boiling water
- ½ cup of milk

Preparation:
1. Put the powdered ingredients in a glass.
2. Add a little boiling water.
3. Stir a little.
4. The powder must dissolve into a thick paste.
5. Fill the rest of the glass with milk.
6. Chill for around 15 minutes.
7. Mix in the ice cream
8. Indulge!

# OREO FRAPPE

Ingredients:

- 1 ¼  cup of crushed ice
- 3 pieces of oreo cookies
- 6 tablespoons of cold espresso
- At least ½ cup of milk
- 1 bar of milk chocolate

Preparation:
1.    Shave the chocolate bar.
2.    Combine the espresso, milk and cookies in a blender.
3.    Add the crushed ice.
4.    Blend until smooth.
5.    Taste the mixture and add more milk if needed.
6.    Pour the mixture into a tall glass.
7.    Decorate the top with the chocolate shavings.
8.    Serve with a fat straw.

# DETOXIFYING SUMMER ICED COFFEE

Ingredients:

- 1 cup of ice cubes
- 1 tablespoon of maca powder
- 2 tablespoons of raw organic cacao powder
- 1 teaspoon of mesquite powder
- 1 teaspoon of lucuma powder
- ½ teaspoon of liquid stevia extract
- 1 tablespoon of vanilla extract
- ½ cup of coconut milk or any other non-dairy milk

Preparation:
1. Mix the stevia and vanilla extracts with the non-dairy milk.
2. Combine all powdered ingredients in a blender.
3. Pour in the milk mixture and the ice.
4. Blend until it looks like a slushie.
5. Pour slushie in a tall chilled glass with a straw.
6. Enjoy your summer and relax!

# fruity ICED COFFEE

Ingredients:

- ½ cup of ice cubes
- 1 banana
- 2 Brazilian nuts
- 4 ½ strips of dried mango
- ½ teaspoon of shredded coconut
- ¼ cup of coconut cream
- 2 tablespoons of peanut butter
- 1 teaspoon of unsalted roasted peanuts
- 3 teaspoons of brown sugar
- ½ teaspoon of cereal or rice crispies.
- 1 shot of cold espresso
- 1 shot of hot espresso
- !T cup of vanilla frozen yogurt or ice cream

Preparation:
1.    Stir the brown sugar into the hot espresso. Let it cool.
2.    While the hot espresso is cooling, chop the Brazilian nuts and dried mango into fine pieces.
3.    Roughly grind the peanuts.
4.    Combine the hot espresso, cold espresso, banana, coconut cream, grounded peanuts, peanut butter, yogurt, ice and brown sugar in a blender.
5.    Blend until smooth.
6.    Pour mixture in a chilled glass.
7.    Stir in the mango and Brazilian nuts.

8.	Top it off with the shredded coconut and cereal or rise crispies.
9.	You may sprinkle other fruits and nuts that you like.
10.	Sit back and enjoy.